Proof that the Bible is

the Word
of God

Jay Wilson, Evangelist
1233 N. 8th
Bozeman, MT 59715
Ph: 406-581-2930, 406-586-8061
www.newcreationstudies.org
www.christschurchonline.com
email: wilsonj@mcn.net

Restoring the ANCIENT ORDER | Developing the NEW CREATION

11th Hour Press

Dear Reader,

This Bible study is the first in a series designed to teach you the basics of the New Testament. It is our prayer that it will accomplish its purpose.

This study is in many senses the most important, for if the Bible is not the word of God, then the New Testament has no important meaning, other than being a "mythological moralizer." I was, at one time, an atheist myself, having come to the conclusion that God was merely the creation of the human mind. But a thorough examination of the scriptures has convinced me that God does in fact exist, and that the Bible is His written revelation to us. This booklet contains the elements of that examination (it will take a much larger book to cover the subject with any degree of completeness). It is a skeleton, which is the beginning place for hanging the meat of more study. But it does contain the elements which prove that the Bible is the word of God, and I trust you will find it interesting and challenging.

The conclusions reached in this study are as follows:

1. The Bible is accurate in dealing with external matters. It is accurate in its record of archeology and natural science. In order to be the word of God, the Bible must be accurate in its portrayal of observable facts. The Bible meets this requirement of accuracy in external matters, and therefore can be the written revelation from God.

2. The proof that the Bible is the word of God comes from its internal contents. The Bible contains the following categories of internal evidence which prove it to be the word of God:

    a) Fulfilled historical prophecies.

    b) Fulfilled predictions of the Messiah.

    c) A Plan revealed, then carefully carried out—proof of the existence of the Planner, and a bridge binding the Old and New Testaments together as one complete unit.

The major point in this study is that the Old Testament is a blueprint and the New Testament is the construction process of a spiritual building, carefully overseen by a Divine Architect.

The New American Standard Version of the Bible was used in the preparation of this study, and is quoted throughout.

Your servant,

Jay Wilson

"The Bible only . . . makes Christians only . . ."

Proof that the Bible is

the Word
of God

Jay Wilson

PROOF THAT THE BIBLE IS THE WORD OF GOD

Introduction:

- The attack on the Bible.
- The purpose of this study is to provide forceful and useful evidence to counter the attack.

Outline:

I. External considerations.
II. Internal evidences.

I. External Considerations

A. *Archeology*

- Joshua and the battle of Jericho (*Halley's Bible Handbook*—Joshua 6)
- Nineveh -"Jonah's Mound" and the library of Assurbanipal (*Halley's Bible Handbook* - Jonah and Nahum)

⟫⟫The Bible contains thousands of details—some of them fantastic. Yet the more we check into these details, the more we find that the Bible is entirely accurate.⟪⟪

B. *Evolution vs. Creation*
- The theory of evolution
- The literal six days of creation
- A time chart
- Some fossil finds
  - Dinosaur and human footprints fossilized at the same time in the Paluxy River bed at Glen Rose, Texas
  - Trilobite crushed by a human sandal, Utah
- Other questions:
  - Uranium dating
  - Age of fossils
  - Mutations
  - Evolution of a primitive cell by random action
  - Second Law of Thermodynamics

⟫⟫The facts of science tend to verify the Bible rather than the theory of evolution.⟪⟪

II. Internal Evidences

A. *Introduction*

- Internal evidences are the only proof that the Bible is God's word; the external considerations are only corroborating evidence.

B. *Historical prophecies*

- Nebuchadnezzar's dream ~ Daniel 2:31-45 (595 BC)
  · Gold ~ Babylon, to 536 BC
  · Silver ~ Media-Persia, from 536 to 333 BC
  · Bronze ~ Greece, from 333 to 200 BC
  · Iron, iron mixed with clay ~ Rome, from 200 BC to AD 400
  · The Stone ~ The Lord's church, from AD 30 to forever
- Daniel's vision of the ram and the goat ~ Daniel 8:1-8;20-22 (545 BC)
  · Ram ~ Media-Persia (larger horn is Persia)
  · Shaggy goat ~ Greece
  · 1st horn on goat ~Alexander the Great
  · The four horns ~ The four generals after the death of Alexander
    - Ptolemy ~ Egypt
    - Seleucus ~ Syria
    - Cassander ~ Macedonia
    - Lysimachus ~ Thrace
- The naming of Cyrus ~ Isaiah 44:28-45:1 (730 BC)
  · Cyrus would allow the Jews to return to destroyed Jerusalem and rebuild the city and lay the foundation of the Temple

>⌒The Bible predicts historic happenings hundreds of years before they take place, giving names and details.⌒<

C. *Fulfilled Messianic Prophecies*

- Isaiah 53 (730 BC)
- Psalm 22:16-18; Psalm 22:1 (1000 BC)
- Details in Christ's life foretold
  · His birth
      ~ Micah 5:2-5
      ~ Isaiah 9:6,7
      ~ Isaiah 7:14
  · His ministry ~ Isaiah 9:1,2
  · His kingdom ~Daniel 2:44,45

· His death ~ Isaiah 53:5-9
· His resurrection ~ Psalm 16:8-10
· His suffering ~ Isaiah 50:6
· His entrance into Jerusalem ~ Zechariah 9:9

Over 150 prophecies of the Old Testament were fulfilled by Jesus in His life, His death, and His resurrection.

D. *The Plan*

• Phase 1

· Genesis 1:26 ~ Man is a spiritual being, with a spiritual need of being in fellowship with God
· Genesis 2:16,17 ~ Adam and Eve lost their fellowship with God
· The Flood ~ Man left to himself becomes degenerate

• Phase 2 ~ Genesis 12:3 – In Abraham all the families of earth would be blessed

• Phase 3 ~ The Law foreshadowed the Christian covenant, containing:
    1. Laws by which the people were to live
    2. Ordinances for sacrifice
    3. The establishment of the priesthood

· The Law contained in itself the seeds of its own destruction
    ~Jeremiah 31:31-34 – Prophecy of the new covenant
    ~Daniel 9:27– Prophecy of the end of old covenant sacrifice
    ~Psalm 110:4 – Prophecy of the establishment of a new priesthood

• Phase 4 ~The establishment of the kings
    · II Samuel 7:16 ~ The promise of an eternal king, descended from David
    · Zechariah 6:12,13 ~ Union of High Priest and King

• Phase 5 ~ The person of Jesus

• Phase 6 ~ The establishment of the church—restoration of fellowship with God, lost since the days of Adam

• Phase 7 ~ Extension of salvation to the Gentiles – Hosea 1:10; Joel 2:32

• Phase 8 ~ Day of Judgment – Malachi 4:1,2; Acts 17:30,31

The Plan is proof of the existence of the Supreme Planner. The Bible reveals a carefully executed design, which is made clear through the church's purpose on earth. This Plan, laid out in prophecy and foreshadow in the Old Testament, and executed in the New, binds the Bible together as one complete unit.

III. Conclusion

The Bible is the word of God for these reasons:

1. The Bible is accurate in dealing with external matters. It is accurate in its record of archeology and natural science. In order to be the word of God, the Bible must be accurate in its portrayal of observable facts. The Bible meets this requirement of accuracy in external matters, and therefore can be the written revelation from God.

2. The proof that the Bible is the word of God comes from its internal contents. The Bible contains the following categories of internal evidence which prove it to be the word of God:

    a) Fulfilled historical prophecies.
    b) Fulfilled predictions of the Messiah.
    c) A Plan revealed, then carefully carried out—proof of the existence of the Planner, and a bridge binding the Old and New Testaments together as one complete unit.

Proof that the Bible is the Word of God

INTRODUCTION

The Bible is being attacked! And please do not be so naive as to believe that the attackers are a few scattered renegades. The big guns of this world, carried by huge warships of evil, are zeroing in on their target, ready to level a blast that will destroy what their admirals have labeled "Organized Religion." Missiles from Satan's abode, laden with explosive warheads of confusion, are already zinging their way to their destination, to obliterate forever the belief that the Bible is the word of God.

For instance, here is a quote from a sociology textbook for elementary college courses: "Sometime between the beginning of the eighteenth century and the end of the nineteenth, God died, though theology could not arrange a formal burial until the 1960's" (*Sociology for a New Day*, Thomas F. Hoult, Random House, 1974; p. 197).

And here is a sample quotation from the *Encyclopedia Americana*: "Geological, anthropological, and archeological study makes it impossible for thinking men to take seriously the Biblical view of the universe and stories of creation in Genesis" (*Encyclopedia Americana*, 1968 Ed.; Vol. 3, p. 689; "The Bible"). The first quotation could be a renegade. But there is no question that the Encyclopedia Americana is a big gun.

Unless defenders of the faith begin a vigorous counter–attack, the American public will rapidly come to believe that the Bible is not the word of God. The proverb is true: fiction repeated often enough becomes fact in the public mind.

The purpose of this study is to present to you simple, yet forceful and useful evidence—proof, in fact!—that the Bible is indeed the absolute and immutable word of God.

OUTLINE

   I. External Considerations

  II. Internal Evidences

I. EXTERNAL CONSIDERATIONS

Archeology

Archeology cannot prove that the Bible is the word of God. But it certainly could provide evidence that either supports the contention that it is, or it can provide evidence that it is not. The fact is that archeology provides evidence that does point to the authorship of the Bible as being Divine. There are thousands of examples that could be used to illustrate how the Bible is corroborated by archeology, but we wish to select just two as representative, the cities of Jericho and Nineveh.

Jericho

The story of Joshua and the battle of Jericho is recorded in Joshua 6 in the Old Testament. Following the 40 years of wandering in the wilderness, the people of Israel crossed the Jordan River under the leadership of Joshua, who replaced Moses as the earthly captain of God's people. Israel prepared to conquer the walled city of Jericho by marching around the city walls once a day for six days. On the seventh day, they marched around the city seven times, and at the blast of a trumpet, the people shouted. According to the Bible account, the walls of the city fell down flat; and the fighting men of Israel, who had the city surrounded, went straight to the center of the city, killing everyone (with the exception of a woman named Rahab, and her family). Then they burned the city with fire.

Here is a strange story. To the so-called thinking man of the 21th century, such stories belong to the realm of mythology. But what is the evidence from archeology?

Dr. John Garstang, director of the British School of Archeology in Jerusalem and of the Department of Antiquities of the Palestine Government, excavated the ruins of Jericho, 1929–1936. He found pottery and scarab evidence that the city had been destroyed about 1400 BC, coinciding with Joshua's date; and in a number of details, dug up evidence confirming the Biblical account in a most remarkable way.

"The wall fell down flat." Dr. Garstang found that the wall did actually 'fall down flat.' The wall was double, the two walls being 15 ft apart; the outer wall , 6 ft thick; the inner wall, 23 ft thick; both being about 30 ft high. They were built, not very substantially, on faulty uneven foundations, of brick 4 inches thick and 1 to 2 ft long, laid in mud mortar. The two walls were linked together by houses built across the top, as Rahab's 'house on the wall.'

Dr. Garstang found that the outer wall fell outwards and down the hillside, dragging the inner wall and houses with it, the streak of bricks gradually getting thinner down the slope. The foundation walls of the palace, 4 courses of stone high, remain, in situ, tilted downward. Dr. Garstang thinks there are indications that the wall was shaken down by an earthquake (of which traces may be seen), a method which God could have used as easily as any other.

"They burnt the city with fire." . . . Signs of the conflagration and destruction were very marked. Garstang found great layers of charcoal and ashes and the wall ruins reddened by fire. "The outer wall suffered most. Houses alongside the wall were burned to the ground. The stratum generally was covered with a deep layer of black burnt debris, under which there were pockets of white ash, overlaid with a layer of fallen reddish brick" (*Halley's Bible Handbook*, Zondervan Press; comments on Joshua 6).

This is solid archeological evidence which verifies the Biblical account. The record, written in the earth 3400 years ago, tells the same story, as nearly as it is possible to determine, as is recorded in the Bible.

Nineveh

We come now to the second of our cities, Nineveh. Nineveh is famous chiefly as being the city to which Jonah was sent after being swallowed and then vomited up by the great fish. Nineveh is described in the Bible as "an exceedingly great city, a three days' walk" (Jonah 3:3), and containing "more than 120,000 persons who do not know the difference between their right and left hands" (Jonah 4:11). A city with 120,000 babies or very small children is a large city even by today's standards.

"So completely had all traces of the glory of the Assyrian Empire [of

3

which Nineveh was the capital] disappeared that many scholars had come to think that the references to it in the Bible and other ancient histories were mythical; and that in reality such a city and such an Empire never existed.

"In 1820 an Englishman, Claude James Rich, spent 4 months sketching the mounds across the Tigris from Mosul, which he suspected were the ruins of Nineveh. In 1845 Layard definitely identified the site; and he and his successors uncovered the ruins of the magnificent palaces of the Assyrian kings, whose names have now become household words, and hundreds of thousands of inscriptions in which we read the history of Assyria as the Assyrians themselves wrote it, and which to a remarkable degree confirm the Bible" (*Halley's Bible Handbook*, Zondervan Press, comments on Nahum).

The scoffers and doubters of the early 1800's were using the lack of secular evidence about Nineveh to try to convince many that the Bible was in error, and that it therefore could not be the word of God. And, as has happened time after time, after further examination, the Bible has been shown to be completely accurate.

Even the story of Jonah is somewhat verified by archeological finds in Nineveh. According to the Bible, Jonah had preached, "Yet forty days, and Nineveh will be overthrown" (Jonah 3:4).

As a result of his preaching, the whole city changed its attitude and behavior, and in consequence God did not destroy the city. If this really happened—if Jonah really had such an impact on such a large city—we would expect to find some evidence of that man's existence. Because of the Bible's accuracy in such matters, we are not surprised when we read, "The second largest mound in Nineveh is called 'Yunas.' 'Yunas' is the native word for 'Jonah.' The mound covers 40 acres and is 100 ft. high. It contains the reputed tomb of Jonah. This was one of the indications to Rich that these were the ruins of Nineveh, and led to their identification" (*Halley's Bible Handbook*, Zondervan Press, comments on Jonah).

Another major find in the ruins of Nineveh was the library of Assurbanipal. "Perhaps the most epochal discovery ever made. Uncovered by Layard, Rassam, and Rawlison, 1852–1854, in the palace of Sennacherib. Originally contained 100,000 volumes. About a third of it has been recovered and is in the British Museum. Assurbanipal was something of an archeologist; had his scribes search and copy the libraries of ancient Babylon, of an age 2000 years before his day. Thus to him we are indebted for preserving knowledge of primitive Babylonian literature" (*Halley's Bible Handbook*, Zondervan Press, comments on Nahum). This library is the source of thousands of details which may be used to verify the Bible account of history for more than 2000 years of ages past.

Summary

We have for our section entitled *Archeology* selected just two cities, Jericho and Nineveh. In both of these we have seen how archeology confirms the Bible record. And this is typical of a long list—Memphis, Babylon, Sidon, and Megiddo, just to name a few—of the cities which the Bible accurately describes. The Bible's accuracy makes it a continuing guide to major archeological finds in the Middle East. If the Bible were merely a collection of legends handed down through the years, there would be numerous errors in it. *The absence of such errors warrants the conclusion that the Bible is more than such a collection.*

Evolution vs. Creation

We now wish to deal with evolution and its relationship to the Bible. Evolution is a widely-believed theory which postulates that life on earth has come to its present state through millions of years of progression from lower forms of life.

In contrast, the Bible states that the earth and its life forms were created in six days some 6000 years ago. The Bible further defines one day as "morning and evening" (Genesis 1:5). Those who believe that the Bible is the word of God are compelled to believe in a literal six days of creation. The voice of God Himself spoke from Mt. Sinai in the giving of the fourth commandment: "For in six days the Lord made the heavens and the earth, the sea and all that is in them, and rested on the seventh day; therefore God blessed the Sabbath day, and made it holy" (Exodus 20:11). In two specific ways the Old Testament defines a "day" of creation as corresponding closely to our normal twenty-four hour day.

Not only that, but the Lord Jesus in the New Testament confirms the shortness of the time of creation. "But from the beginning of creation, God made them male and female" (Mark 10:6). If it had taken man a long time to come into existence after creation was initiated, then man and woman would not have been there at the time Jesus called "the beginning of creation." A person who believes in the Bible is forced to believe in a literal six days of creation.

If evolution is correct, the Bible obviously is not the literal word of God. And, as a matter of fact, widespread belief in evolution is one of the major reasons why many people do not believe in the Bible.

Consider the scope of evolution (see Figure 1). Evolution is rooted in the concept that the earth began four to five *billion* years ago when material in the universe, such as a giant dust cloud, came together to form a swirling, molten ball. Over a period of three to four billion years this molten ball cooled down.

By one billion years ago the earth was covered with a seething solution of water, ammonia, and related chemicals, bubbling with methane gas. This brew is known as the "primeval broth." All the chemicals necessary for life were present in exactly the right amounts at exactly the right temperature. Then lightning (or some other stimulus) struck the mixture, the chemicals came together in exactly the right combinations, and life began as a primitive cell started to function.

From this primitive cell different life forms began to evolve. By 500 million years ago primitive plants had evolved, as well as primitive animals related to clams and snails. One of the most predominant forms of these shelled animals was the trilobite. Trilobites existed from 500 million to 300 million years ago, and then they died out (*Encyclopedia Americana*, 1968 Ed.; Vol. 21, pp. 186–194; *Paleontology*).

By 200 million years ago reptiles had replaced these earlier crustaceans as the dominant form of life. The giant reptiles, the dinosaurs, lumbered over the earth, unchallenged as kings, for 140 million years. With the shift in climate, reptiles such as these were unable to compete with the rapidly evolving mammals, and by 60 million years ago, the age of dinosaurs had drawn to a close as the last of the "terrible lizards" wheezed his last breath.

The Cenozoic Era is the age of mammals. This Era began 60 million years ago and has lasted up to the present. By the beginning of this age primitive mammals had begun to evolve, and by the middle of the Era giant mammals nearly as large as dinosaurs roamed over the earth. Step by step each group of mammals gave way to a more advanced form, until one million years ago *homo sapiens*, modern man, appeared on the scene. Today he totally dominates the earth, and will continue to do so until he gives way to a higher form of life.

The Bible, in contrast, teaches that the earth began some 6000 years ago, and that all animals and plants were formed in the beginning. Following the Flood, which occurred roughly 4500 years ago, the climate of the earth was apparently radically changed, and many forms of life which once existed became extinct.

Having presented these two views concerning the origin of man, we want to consider some very pertinent facts. And we want to see which view—Bible Creation or Evolution—is more consistent with these facts.

Fact Number 1: Near Glen Rose, Texas, in the bed of the Paluxy River, are fossilized dinosaur tracks. That is not surprising, because dinosaur tracks are found in many places throughout the world. What is surprising is that human footprints are fossilized in the same rock stratum, with some of the human tracks fossilized as actually stepping into the dinosaur tracks. (There is some controversy currently concerning the human tracks in the Paluxy. Because the tracks themselves are a powerful refutation of evolution, the controversy is not unexpected. You will need to see them yourself.)

According to evolutionary theory, dinosaurs died out 60 million years before man, with his distinctive footprint, walked on the face of the earth. But here is a fact, preserved in stone for anyone to see, proving that man and dinosaur lived at the same time. Furthermore, the limestone edge which must be ripped away to get to some of the tracks makes it clear that the tracks are of "normal dinosaur age."

Figure 1.

TIME CHARTS ACCORDING TO EVOLUTION AND CREATION

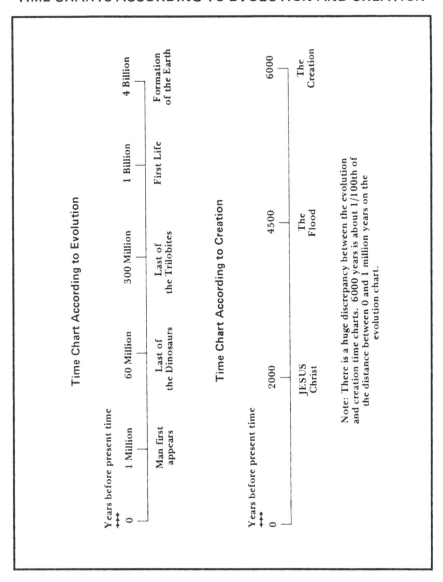

Time Chart According to Evolution

Years before present time

0	1 Million	60 Million	300 Million	1 Billion	4 Billion
	Man first appears	Last of the Dinosaurs	Last of the Trilobites	First Life	Formation of the Earth

Time Chart According to Creation

Years before present time

0	2000	4500	6000
	JESUS Christ	The Flood	The Creation

Note: There is a huge discrepancy between the evolution and creation time charts. 6000 years is about 1/100th of the distance between 0 and 1 million years on the evolution chart.

This fact—that man and dinosaur lived at the same time—is a bull in the evolutionary china closet. It wrecks everything! If man existed with dinosaurs, then man did not evolve from dinosaurs. And if man did not evolve from dinosaurs, then neither did the other mammals. And if mammals did not evolve from dinosaurs, this throws that "most accurate" portion of the evolutionary chart out the window. And with the "most accurate" portion of evolution gone, the "less accurate" portion of the chart, from "first life" down to dinosaurs, is extremely questionable.

But notice that the Bible model, stating that all things lived together at the beginning, predicts that we should find evidence of both man and dinosaur living at the same time in the same place.

Fact Number 2: "George Howe in the *Creation Research Quarterly* of December 1968 reports the find of William Meister in Utah of a sandal footprint with crushed trilobites in it!" (*The Christ and the Intertestament Period*, Wartick and Fields, College Press, Joplin, MO; "The Christian and Evolution," p. 686).

According to evolutionary theory, trilobites died out some 300 million years ago. According to the Bible, trilobites and man lived at the same time. That fact that a living trilobite was crushed by a human sandal, then fossilized, is hard to explain unless the Bible is true.

Other Questions: What about the fossil record, uranium dating, mutations, and other items discovered by science which are generally accepted as verifying evolution? All of these are discussed very completely in an excellent book written by a group of eminent scientists, and edited by Henry M. Morris of the Institute for Creation Research, entitled *Scientific Creationism* (published by Creation-Life Publishers, San Diego, CA 92115).

1. The use of radioactive uranium and its decay into lead as a means of dating the age of the earth at 4.5 billion years is invalid because of certain assumptions which are basic to the method (that all lead in the sample was derived from the original uranium is one of the assumptions). For example, in testing the ages of some lava rocks,

it was found that "most of them gave ages of over a billion years, even though the lava rocks were known to have been formed in modern times" (p. 143).

2. Rocks are usually dated by the kinds of fossils found in them or in rock layers near them. The age of a fossil is determined by its complexity—simple fossils are assumed to be old, and complex fossils are assumed to be more recent. "The fossils speak of evolution because they have been made to speak of evolution" (p. 96).

3. Mutation, the mechanism upon which evolution depends for one form to evolve into a higher form, is always harmful rather than helpful. ". . . a truly beneficial mutation . . . has yet to be documented" (p. 56).

4. Even a simple cell could not have been formed by the mechanics of random action in 30 billion years (p. 62).

5. The Second Law of Thermodynamics states that everything in the universe is tending toward decay, or disorder. For instance, in accordance with the Second Law of Thermodynamics, each year it takes the earth a small fraction of a second longer to make its annual revolution around the sun.

   The Second Law also applies to living systems. Because the Law forces all things toward decay or degeneration, it is impossible for there to be any long-term upgrading from lower life forms to more advanced forms. "We are warranted, then, in concluding that the evolutionary process . . . is completely precluded by the Second Law of Thermodynamics" (p. 45).

It is interesting that the Bible is entirely consistent with the Second Law of Thermodynamics, even going so far as to make a word statement of it: "For the creation was *subjected to futility*, not of its own will, but because of Him who subjected it, in hope that the creation itself also will be set free from its *slavery to corruption*. . ." (Romans 8:20,21). The Second Law predicts no new life forms, and general decay from a good beginning. So does the Bible: "And God saw all that He had made, and behold, it was very good" (Genesis 1:31).

The conclusion is apparent: evolution does not invalidate the Bible. Rather, the *facts* connected with the fossil record and natural science are consistent with the Bible, and tend to verify it rather than evolution.

Summary

In our discussion concerning the Bible as the word of God, we have discussed two subjects, archeology and evolution. The Bible can be shown to be accurate in regard to archeology, which points to divine authorship of its history. And the facts of natural science, rather than relegating the Bible to the realms of mythology as is widely assumed, tend to verify the Bible's accuracy!

II. INTERNAL EVIDENCES

Introduction

We have seen that archeology and natural science tend to verify the Bible. However, the evidence from these is merely supportive, and not proof. The real evidence that the Bible is the word of God must be internal.

Why must proof that the Bible is the word of God be internal? It is clear, upon reflection, that it would be possible for a human being to write a book without error. The test of the accuracy of such a book would be to compare it to reality. For example, if a book states that water boils at 212° F at sea level, that can be tested by going to sea level and boiling water. To prove, then, that a book such as the Bible is accurate in comparison to external considerations is not proof that the book is authored by God. It is necessary evidence, but it is not sufficient for proof. The evidence which is sufficient will come in internal evidences which the human mind cannot duplicate.

Of what would this internal proof consist? An old homesteader's shack, now partially fallen down, is proof of the one–time existence of the home-steader. The design, clearly not by chance, is proof of the existence of the designer. In the same way, proof of the existence of God would be a transcendent design, carried out on a scale which chance or human planning could not duplicate.

Does the Bible offer such a transcendent design? We will find the Bible clearly shows that its authorship is something beyond human in its predictions of history, its predictions of the Messiah, and its setting forth and carrying out a grand design. We will find that the Bible reveals a Plan carried out without wavering over thousands of years—proof which binds the Bible together as one complete unit.

Fulfilled Historical Prophecy

Historical prophecy begins very early in the Bible. In Genesis 15, according to the Bible record, God foretold that Abraham's descendants would be enslaved in a foreign land for 400 years, but that they would come out of that land with many possessions—a prophecy of Israel's enslavement and delivery from Egypt.

Other prophecies were given as the Bible account continued its journey through history. For example, before Moses' ascension of Mt. Nebo to die, he pronounced a blessing upon the people of Israel if the people kept the Law; but if they broke the Law, he promised that the Lord would curse the people. In the promised curses recorded in Deuteronomy, he foretold the coming of a time when they would have a king (Deuteronomy 28:36), and their destruction at the hands of the merciless Assyrians and Babylonians (Deuteronomy 28:49–68). Such prophecies were fulfilled hundreds of years later.

We have chosen to consider three historical prophecies from the Old Testament as representative and instructive of the authorship of God.

Our first example is from Daniel 2. Daniel as a young man was brought captive from Jerusalem to Babylon when his homeland was conquered by the Babylonian king Nebuchadnezzar. Because of the wisdom and knowledge which Daniel possessed, he with three other youths was assigned office with the soothsayers and magicians of Babylon (Daniel 1:1–21).

In the second year of Nebuchadnezzar's reign over Jerusalem, the king had a dream which troubled him, and he anxiously desired to know the meaning of the dream. Calling his master astrologers (the Chaldeans) together, he issued a command: "... if you do not make known to me the dream and its interpretation, you will be torn limb from limb ..." (Daniel 2:5).

The Chaldeans, of course, having no idea at all what the dream was, begged the king to tell them the contents of the dream. If the king would only do that, they would tell him the meaning of the dream. But Nebuchadnezzar, one of the craftiest, most able kings of all time, did not trust the astrologers and sorcerers. He told them, "For you have agreed together to speak lying and corrupt words before me until the situation is changed; therefore tell me the dream, that I may know that you can declare to me the interpretation" (Daniel 2:9).

As expected, none of the magicians or Chaldeans could tell the king what the dream was. Orders went forth to kill all the so-called wise men, including Daniel and his three friends. When Daniel found out what was going on, he asked the king for a little time, and prayed to God that He would make known to Daniel the dream and its interpretation, so that his life would be spared. The Lord, according to the Bible, granted his request.

We next find Daniel in the presence of the king. After giving God all the credit for the dream and its interpretation, Daniel first told the king what the dream was, so that the king would know that Daniel was telling the truth about the interpretation. The central figure in the dream was a statue, described as having a head of gold, breast and arms of silver, belly and thighs of bronze, legs of iron and feet of iron and clay. Then a stone, cut out of a mountain without hands, struck the statue on the feet and smashed it to smithereens. Following this, a wind came up and blew the pieces of the statue away; but the stone which struck the statue became a great mountain which filled the whole earth (Daniel 2:31–35).

In Daniel 2:36–45, Daniel gives the king the interpretation. The head of gold is Babylon, with Nebuchadnezzar as king. Then came a silver kingdom, followed by a bronze kingdom. Finally came a fourth kingdom, described as strong as iron, but divided. In the days of these iron kings, God is described as setting up His kingdom, which would never be destroyed. And Daniel makes it clear that God's kingdom is represented by the stone, which destroyed the other kingdoms.

It is easy to trace the path of Daniel's prophecy through time. The Babylonians lasted until 536 BC; then came the Medes and Persians, who were partners. The Medes and Persians dominated until 333 BC, when the Greeks, represented by the bronze, replaced them. The Greeks were progressively overthrown by the iron of Rome, with Roman domination being complete by 200 BC.

Liberal and conservative theologians alike both usually stumble over the fact that the kingdom of God, as viewed by the Bible, is the church (see the study on "The Church as the Kingdom of God" in the booklet *Christ's Church*), and are unable to unravel the meaning of this prophecy of Daniel's. But it is clear that the church was begun by God, and not man, just as the stone in the vision (which represented the kingdom of God, Daniel 2:44,45) was cut out without human hands. It is clear that the church, which began on the day of Pentecost, AD 30, was set up in the days of the Roman, or iron, kings. And it is clear that, just as the stone became a mountain which filled the whole earth, so the church will increase and will go to the ends of the earth. And someday the kingdom of this world will "become the kingdom of our Lord and of His Christ; and He will reign forever and ever" (Revelation 11:15), and the prophecy of Daniel will finally be completely fulfilled.

The description of the iron kingdom as being divided, partly of iron and partly of clay, is a good description of the Roman Empire in New Testament times. For example, when Jesus was born, Augustus Caesar was Emperor, Herod the Great was king, and there were various governors scattered throughout. These men were always jockeying for position, and the local rulers did not mix well with the Romans, as pottery does not mix with iron. But everywhere was the toughness of iron, the Roman army.

If we accept Biblical dating for this writing in Daniel, Nebuchadnezzar saw this vision sometime between 605 BC and 585 BC. Some 600 years before God set up His kingdom, Daniel, in a prophetic panorama, predicted the coming of three empires following the Babylonians, culminating in God's kingdom. Furthermore, he predicted that God's kingdom would spread throughout the whole earth, and that it would last forever. If the Bible date for this writing is correct, there is only one explanation—God knew what was going to happen ahead of time, and He wrote it down for us scoffers and doubters, and those of us of little faith.

The Ram and the Goat

Let's consider another prophetic vision of Daniel, given in Daniel 8:1–8. Daniel, again according to Bible dating, received this vision near 545 BC, as Belshazzar was in his third year as king of Babylon (probably as co-regent). In this vision Daniel himself was placed in a different location; he was removed to Persia. He saw a ram with two horns (the second horn coming up longer) butting north, west, and south. Then from the west came a male goat, with one big horn between its eyes, and he smashed the ram and trampled him into the dirt. Then the big horn was broken off, and in its place came four horns.

This part of Daniel's vision is interpreted in Daniel 8:20–22. We are told that the shaggy goat represented Greece, and the ram represented the kingdom of Media-Persia. The large horn in the middle of the goat's head was the Greek Empire's first king, and the four horns which arose after the larger horn was broken off represented the four kingdoms which arose out of the first king's power.

It is amazing how descriptive Daniel's vision is. The Medes and the Persians were partners. The Medes dominated at first, but the Persians eventually came to dominate, and they were stronger than the Medes had ever been. This was pictured by the two horns on the ram; the second one, representing

15

the Persians, came up longer (stronger). The Persian Empire was spreading in all directions but east, as foretold by the ram's butting north, west, and south. Then in 333 BC, more than 200 years following Daniel's prophecy, Greece (pictured by the male goat) smashed Persia's power. In ten short years, Alexander the Great, portrayed as the large horn, extended Greek domain to the Indus River in what is now Pakistan. No wonder the billygoat is visualized as moving so fast his feet were not touching the ground; he was flying!

Following Alexander's death in 322 BC, his kingdom was eventually divided among four generals: Ptolemy, Seleucus, Cassander, and Lysimachus. This was prophesied by Daniel in the description of the large horn between the goat's eyes being broken off, and being replaced by four horns.

If we accept the Bible's date for this vision, there is only one explanation for the accuracy and detail which were written down more than 200 years before the events occurred: God knew what was going to happen ahead of time, and He wrote it down for us scoffers and doubters, and those of us of little faith.

The Coming of Cyrus

Our third example of historical prophecy is taken from the book of Isaiah. Isaiah lived and prophesied from 740 to 700 BC. In 605 BC the Babylonians came and conquered his beloved country, Judah, and its capital, Jerusalem (you need this history to understand this prophecy of Isaiah). In 585 BC, because of an extremely rebellious attitude on the part of the Jews, the Babylonians destroyed Jerusalem, wrecked the temple of Solomon, and killed nearly all of Judah's inhabitants. Fifty years later the Medes and the Persians, under King Cyrus of Persia and General Darius the Mede, captured Babylon. It was the policy of Cyrus to allow captive peoples, such as the Jews, to return to their homelands.

More than 175 years before the capture of Babylon, Isaiah wrote: "It is I [the Lord] who says of Cyrus, 'He is My shepherd! And he will perform all My desire. And he declares of Jerusalem, "She shall be built." And of the temple, "Your foundation will be laid." ' Thus says the Lord to Cyrus His anointed" (Isaiah 44:28–45:1).

Before Cyrus was born, according to the Bible, God (through Isaiah) named him by name, and foretold what he was going to do. As the Lord had declared, Cyrus allowed the city of Jerusalem to be rebuilt, and the foundation of the Temple to be re-laid, following their destruction by the Babylonians. Again, if Bible dating is true, there is only one explanation: God, knowing 200 years ahead of time what was going to happen, wrote it down for us scoffers and doubters, and those of us of little faith.

Some Discussion

Daniel's prediction of the four coming kingdoms in the first vision, his description of the Medo-Persian Empire and the coming of Alexander the Great in the second vision, and Isaiah's prophecy about Cyrus of Persia, are very accurate and descriptive. Such accuracy is recognized by all who examine the work, liberal and conservative alike. Those who deny that the Bible is the word of God make such statements as this about the book of Daniel, for example: "The impression that the predictions made in the distant past had been fulfilled so accurately was made possible by the fact that the apocalypses were written after the events had taken place, but they are presented as though they had been made prior to these events" (*Cliff's Notes*, "Old Testament"; Charles H. Patterson, p. 86).

Modern scholars charge that the Bible has been "doctored" to make its prophecies come true. Many believe that the original writings of such books as Genesis and Exodus were from a source labeled "J". Sometime later writings from another source labeled "E" were added, followed by "D" writings. Finally, the whole work was re-edited by the priesthood, and additions labeled "P" made the first five books complete. Later writings from the prophets were added, and the much altered, compacted, deleted, and expanded work (according to modern liberal scholars) is our Old Testament (*Cliff's Notes*, "Old Testament"; Charles H. Patterson, pp. 58,59).

An examination of such charges will reveal that such statements as "the fact that the apocalypses [of Daniel] were written after these events had taken place" are not fact at all! All such charges, although clothed in language designed to convince you that they are based on bedrock truth, are nothing

17

more than conjecture at best, and outright lies at worse. Here is another example: *"Now there is almost universal agreement among Biblical scholars that the Pentateuch [the first five books of the Old Testament] is composed of at least four separate and distinct narratives, written by different persons who were widely separated in point of time (Ibid., p. 56) [emphasis added].* Who these "Biblical scholars" are, and what overwhelming evidence there is for this conclusion is never stated.

What is the point we are trying to make? Simply this: the historical prophecies in the Old Testament are so accurate that those who wish to deny that they were written by God are forced to say that they were written after the events prophesied occurred, without evidence for such conjectures. This sort of speculation may temporarily get them out of a jam, but we will see shortly that these foundationless guesses will smash under the weight of Messianic prophecy.

Of course, if these visions and prophecies were really received at the Biblical dates assigned to them, there is only one possible explanation: they were given by God, and recorded for eternity by His prophets, as proof of His divine authorship.

Fulfilled Messianic Prophecy

For centuries the Jews had awaited the coming of the Messiah to save them. The word Messiah is the Hebrew word meaning "the anointed one." Its Greek equivalent is *christos*, which is where our word Christ comes from. Its meaning is derived from the practice of anointing kings. For example, when God chose David to be king of Israel (the David who killed Goliath), He sent the prophet Samuel down to the house of Jesse. "Fill your horn with oil and go . . . you shall anoint for Me the one whom I designate" (I Samuel 16:1,3). So Samuel filled his horn with oil, and anointed David as king of Israel by pouring the oil on David's head—the anointing—as God instructed. The Messiah, then, was to be the king who was to sit on David's throne, ruling over the house of Jacob.

The Jews expected a Messiah to come because of a large number of prophecies concerning Him. Let's look at some of these prophecies.

The complete text of Isaiah was found among the Dead Sea Scrolls in 1947, and that text is dated at 100 BC (*Encyclopedia Americana*; Vol.3, p. 659; "Bible"; 1968 Ed.). The find has proven to be very significant in that it shows that our present Old Testament, translated from Massoretic texts dated at AD 800, has essentially no differences from texts dated 900 years earlier. In other words, the large number of "copy errors and inclusion of notes into the body of the text" expected by liberal scholars simply were not there. This is strong evidence that the Bible has come to us unchanged through the centuries. Secondly, the book of Isaiah was clearly written in its entirety before the man Jesus came into existence on earth, which provides some interesting dilemmas for those who do not believe that the Bible is the word of God.

In Isaiah 53, the following predictions, written before Christ, are made of a man:

1. He would not be outstanding in appearance (vs. 2).

2. He would be a man of sorrow (vs. 3).

3. He would bear our griefs and sorrows (vs. 4).

4. He would be pierced through for our sins (vs. 5).

5. All of us have gone astray, but God caused the iniquity of us all to fall on this man (vs. 6).

6. He would not try to defend Himself against His accusers (vs. 7).

7. He would be cut off out of the land of the living (He would be killed) for the sins of God's people (vs. 8).

8. Although innocent, His grave would be assigned to be with the wicked, yet He would be with a rich man in His death (vs. 9).

9. He would be offered as a guilt offering, yet somehow would see His offspring, and His days would be prolonged (vs. 10).

10. He, the righteous One, would justify many (vs. 11).

11. He would be greatly rewarded for being poured out to death, and for being numbered with the transgressors (vs. 12).

Such prophecies are a remarkable foreshadow of the Jesus of the New Testament. The New Testament claims for this Jesus are that He came, as the Lamb of God (John 1:29), to be offered for the sins of all men. The New Testament claims that He did not try to defend Himself against His accusers (like a sheep before its shearers). The New Testament claims that He was hung on a cross between two thieves (with the wicked in His death). The New Testament claims that He was pierced through, with a Roman spear, for the transgressions of all men. The New Testament claims that He was buried in the tomb of rich Joseph of Arimathea (with a rich man in His death). The New Testament claims that He was raised from the dead to live forever (that His days would be prolonged), and that He is seated at the right hand of God as King Jesus (greatly rewarded for being poured out to death), watching over His spiritual offspring.

Those who deny that the Bible is the word of God are forced to long wordy explanations in order to try to modify rather clear scripture. The central question obviously in the back of their minds is: "How can I make people think that Isaiah is not talking about Jesus?" For example, in *Cliff's Notes*, the author tries to diffuse the suffering of the Messiah described in Isaiah 53 by applying the suffering to a whole group of people: "In a series of poems called 'Songs of the Suffering Servant,' the prophet sets forth his greatest contribution to Israel's religious ideals. It is here that he points out the purpose and opportunity that lie behind *the unmerited suffering on the part of comparatively innocent persons*" (*Cliff's Notes*; "Old Testament"; Charles H. Patterson, p. 50) [emphasis added].

The objective mind realizes that such specific predictions as Isaiah made are not possible in the realm of the natural; such predictions belong in the realm of the supernatural. Here is strong evidence that the Bible was written by a clearly Supreme Mind.

In Psalm 22:16–18, the crucifixion of someone is very clearly portrayed. "For dogs have surrounded me; a band of evildoers has encompassed me; they pierced my hands and my feet." This crucifixion is especially interesting since crucifying people was not a Jewish practice. The Jewish way was death by stoning.

"I can count all my bones." Whoever this is happening to does not have any broken bones. They did not break Jesus' bones; they did break the bones of the thieves with which He was hanging. But He was dead when the Roman soldiers arrived, and it was not necessary for them to kill Him on the cross.

"They look, they stare at me; they divide my garments among them, and for my clothing they cast lots." This is a perfect description of what the Roman soldiers did with Jesus' belongings as He hung in agony overhead (Matthew 27:33–54).

David wrote this Psalm 1000 years before Jesus was born. And David was not crucified. Whoever this Psalm is about died a Roman death. Whoever this Psalm is about cried out, "My God, My God, why hast Thou forsaken me?" (Psalm 22:1; Matthew 27:46).

If Jesus were just pretending to be the Messiah, you would think that He would stop short of being crucified. After all, life is short enough without that sort of thing. Unless He knew ahead of time that He was going to be raised from the dead—in which case He would not have to pretend that He was the Messiah.

Details in Christ's Life Foretold

We have looked at prophecies concerning the Christ from Isaiah 53 and Psalm 22 in some detail. We now want to list some of the prophecies about the life of the Messiah:

1. **His birth**—Micah 5:2–5 predicts that the ruler of Israel would be born in Bethlehem. "But as for you, Bethlehem Ephrathah [Ephrathah is the old name for Bethlehem, and describes that area], too little to be among the clans of Judah, from you One will go forth

21

for Me to be ruler in Israel. His goings forth are from long ago, from the days of eternity." Furthermore, this ruler in Israel had existed from the days of eternity, and He had appeared a number of times prior to His birth. This passage of scripture goes on to describe the lost condition of Israel prior to the coming of the Messiah, and how the "shepherd king" would eventually be great throughout the whole earth. "Therefore He [God] will give them up until the time when she who is in labor has born a child. Then the remainder of His brethren will return to the sons of Israel. And He will arise and shepherd His flock in the strength of the Lord, and the majesty of the name of the Lord His God. And they will remain, because at that time He will be great to the ends of the earth."

— Isaiah 9:6,7 tells us that a son would be born to sit on the throne of David. "For a child will be born to us, a son will be given to us; and the government will rest on His shoulders; and His name will be called Wonderful Counselor [the Holy Spirit], Mighty God, eternal Father, Prince of Peace. There will be no end to the increase of His government or of peace, on the throne of David and over his kingdom . . ." The Old Testament predicts that all of God would be Christ, and in Christ. Such characteristics are precisely what Jesus claimed for Himself, and what the apostles attributed to Him after His resurrection (John 14:6,7 – Jesus is the Father; John 8:58 – Jesus is the Mighty God; John 14:16,17 – Jesus is the Holy Spirit; Colossians 1:19 – It was the Father's good pleasure for all the fullness to dwell in him).

— Isaiah 7:14 prophesies that "God with us" would be born of a virgin.

2. **His ministry**—Isaiah 9:1,2 promises that Jesus would spend most of His time near the Sea of Galilee, the region belonging to the tribes of Zebulun and Naphtali in the original apportionment of the promised land among the twelve tribes of Israel. This area by

Isaiah's time had long since lapsed into idolatry, hence described as being in darkness. Of the land of Zebulun and Naphtali, God says through Isaiah, "The people who walk in darkness will see a great light; those who live in a dark land, the light will shine on them."

3. **His kingdom**—We have already seen how, from Daniel 2:44,45, God would set up His kingdom in the days of the Roman kings. Isaiah 9:7 shows that the child born would be the One sitting on the throne in that kingdom.

4. **His death**—We have already seen from Isaiah 53:5–9 how the Redeemer would be pierced through for the people's sins, and that He would be cut off out of the land of the living for their transgressions.

5. **His resurrection**—Psalm 16 contains a prophecy of the Christ's resurrection. In verse 8 the Father speaks of the Son as being at His right hand, "I have set the Lord continually before me; because He is at my right hand, I will not be shaken." Then the Son speaks, "Therefore my heart is glad, and my glory rejoices; my flesh also will dwell securely. For Thou wilt not abandon my soul to Sheol; neither wilt Thou allow Thy Holy One to undergo decay" (Psalm 16:9–10). The Holy One was going to go to *Sheol* [Greek—*Hades*], the resting place of the soul following death. However, this One's soul was not going to be abandoned to Sheol, and He was not going to be dead long enough for His flesh to see decay (the pit).

6. **His suffering**—Isaiah prophesies the suffering of the Messiah: "I gave My back to those who strike Me, and My cheeks to those who pluck out the beard; I did not cover My face from humiliation and spitting" (Isaiah 50:6).

7. **His entrance into Jerusalem**—"Rejoice greatly, O daughter of Zion! Shout in triumph, O daughter of Jerusalem! Behold, your king is coming to you; He is just and endowed with salvation,

humble and mounted on a donkey, even on a colt, the foal of a donkey" (Zechariah 9:9). Not only was the king coming in on a donkey, but *He was endowed with salvation*!

These seven details in the life of Jesus illustrate the extent to which the Old Testament proclaims the truthfulness of the New Testament record. Jesus, for instance, could have rigged the riding of a donkey into Jerusalem, if He were smart enough. But there is no probable way to really arrange for Roman soldiers to gamble for clothing just to fulfill some writings 1000 years old, while you conveniently hang on a cross overhead—unless it has been ordained by God. And there is no possible way to come back from the dead in a resurrection, unless that has been pre-arranged by God also.

We have, in this section, listed only a few of the Old Testament prophecies pertaining to Jesus. There are at least 150 specific prophecies concerning a man who was to come, all of which were clearly fulfilled by the Jesus of the New Testament. The number and scope of such prophecies are far beyond the range of human arrangement. There is really only one possible explanation—Divine planning and action. Such Messianic prophecy is some of the strongest proof that the Bible is indeed the word of God and the story of Jesus.

The Plan

Old Testament prophecies prove that the Author of the prophecies is also the Author of history. Prophecies of history prove that the Old Testament is the word of God. The Old Testament prophecies also prove that Jesus is the Christ, the Messiah, and that Matthew, Mark, Luke, and John are the word of God. Since most of the New Testament—the book of Acts, the epistles, and Revelation—relates to the church, and indirectly to Jesus, the question is: Is all of the New Testament the word of God? Another way of asking the same question is: Is part of the Bible the word of God, and part of it merely the word of men? Did the early church "make up" parts of the New Testament to justify its existence?

In this section, we intend to show that, because of *The Plan*, the entire New Testament is the word of God, and that the Bible as a whole is one complete, inspired unit.

24

Phase 1

The Plan begins at the beginning. According to the Bible, God said, "Let us make man in Our image . . ." (Genesis 1:26). Man, made in the image of God (who is Spirit—John 4:24), is a spirit being—different from animals, with spiritual needs. One of those needs is fellowship with God.

When Adam and Eve sinned in the Garden of Eden, they died (Genesis 2:17)—they lost their fellowship with God. At that point, according to the Bible, God began implementing the Plan. Animal sacrifices now began to be offered in atonement for sins.

But, in spite of sacrifices, mankind degenerated rapidly from The Fall, and it became necessary for God to essentially destroy the human race in the Flood of Noah's day. Following the Flood, God said, "I will never again curse the ground on account of man, for the intent of man's heart is evil from his youth; and I will never again destroy every living thing, as I have done" (Genesis 8:21). The lesson of the Flood is that men left to themselves become absolutely corrupt.

Phase 2

Following the Flood, God implemented Phase 2 of the Plan. Dealing with a faithful man named Abram (later Abraham), God promised him, "In you *all the families of earth* shall be blessed" (Genesis 12:3). So from Abraham the Hebrew came the Israelites, who took their name from Jacob (whom God renamed Israel), Abraham's grandson. The Israelites grew into a mighty nation in the land of Egypt, where they settled in the land of Goshen.

But here, at the beginning of the nation Israel, we have God making a promise to bless every family on earth through Abraham. Note that this is an "un-Jewish" thing to write. There are those who maintain that Israel's religion and theology developed as their great thinkers thought new thoughts and added to Jewish tradition. Furthermore, many have the idea that the priests, following the Babylonian captivity of 605 to 536 BC, edited the Old Testament works so as to exalt the priestly position. If these positions were true, given Jewish non-acceptance of the Gentiles, we would never find Genesis 12:3 with its promise of God's blessing on all the families of earth. But here it is, a clear foundation piece of a definite plan for God to do something special for all peoples through Abraham.

Phase 3

Then, through Moses, after the people of Israel had been in Egypt for 400 years, Phase 3 was put into effect. The people of Israel crossed the Red Sea to the wilderness of Sinai where they were given the Law. The Law incorporated three things:

1. Laws by which the people were to live.
2. Regulations for sacrifices offered by the priests (the service), and worship by the Jews in general.
3. The establishment of the priesthood.

From the beginning the Law of Moses was designed to eventually be destroyed, and to be replaced by a superior system:

1. The people would not keep the Law.
2. The regulations for sacrifice, including the design of the Hebrew tabernacle, were designed to foreshadow elements of the Christian religion (see Hebrews chapters 8–10).
3. The priesthood was to foreshadow the priesthood of the Christ, the eternal High Priest.

Not only are these points brought out by Christian authors in the New Testament, but they are manifested in Old Testament prophecy as well:

1. " 'Behold, days are coming,' declares the Lord, 'when I will make a *new covenant* with the house of Israel and the house of Judah; not like the covenant which I made with their fathers in the day I took them by the hand to bring them out of the land of Egypt, *My covenant which they broke*, although I was a husband to them,' declares the Lord" (Jeremiah 31:31,32).

    Jeremiah makes two points here: a) The people would not keep the Law—they broke the covenant which God made with them through Moses; b) God was going to make a new covenant with them which would be different from the one given on Mt. Sinai. It would also be a superior covenant. "I will put My law within them, and on their heart I will write it" (Jeremiah 31:33).

2. "And He [Messiah the Prince] will make a firm covenant with many for one week but in the middle of the week He will put a stop to sacrifice and grain offering . . ." (Daniel 9:27).

Daniel points out that in the middle of a week (a week of years is seven years—a Jewish week could be seven days or seven years—and the middle of a week is three and one-half years), the Messiah would put a stop to Old Testament service, with its grain offerings and sacrifices. If the Messiah were the perfect sacrifice Himself, offered as a guilt offering for the transgressions of all men, His death would certainly put a stop to the other offerings and sacrifices—there would be no more need for them. And it is interesting that the Messiah was cut off after ministering three and one–half years on earth, exactly in accordance with Daniel's prophecy.

3. "The Lord has sworn and will not change His mind, 'Thou art a priest forever according to the order of Melchizedek' " (Psalm 110:4).

Priests of the Mosaic covenant were of the order of Aaron (descended from Moses' brother Aaron) and were of the tribe of Levi. The new priest would be of the order of Melchizedek (Genesis 14:17–24), and He would be a priest forever! Just as the Old Testament pointed to the cessation of sacrifices and offerings, so it also pointed to a change in the priesthood—a priesthood of One who would be a priest forever!

Here's the point: from its very foundation the Israelite religion was designed to be set aside and replaced by a new religion with superior law, superior service and worship, and a superior priesthood. Ask yourself a question: What man, if he were to design a religion, would design it to self-destruct (especially the priesthood)? Ask yourself another question: What man, if he did design a religion to self-destruct, could guarantee the destruction of that religion, and the formation of the superior religion out of it *1400 years later*?

Of course, in history, we find that the real core of the Israelite religion is gone. There is no temple, no priesthood, no sacrifices. In AD 70 all these were swept aside, as Jesus predicted, by the hands of the Romans. All that is left is the written record of the teaching ordinances which no Jew today can follow.

All this points to the existence of a transcendent Designer carrying out His plan through the ages, and revealing it to man through His written word.

Phase 4

For three and one-half centuries Israel had no king; it was governed by judges. The people demanded to have a king like the other nations around them, so God gave Samuel the prophet orders to anoint Saul of the tribe of Benjamin as king. When Saul turned away from God, David the shepherd boy of Bethlehem became the new king, and Phase 4 of God's plan was under way. God promised King David, "And your house and your kingdom shall endure before Me forever; your throne shall be established forever" (II Samuel 7:16). So the Messiah, the Child who was to be born, was to sit on the throne of David forever (Isaiah 9:6,7; Luke 1:32,33).

Not only was the Messiah to be king, according to the Old Testament, but He also would be High Priest. "Thus says the Lord of hosts, 'Behold, a man whose name is Branch, for He will branch out from where He is; and He will build the temple of the Lord . . . and He . . . will bear the honor and sit and rule on His throne. Thus, He will be a priest on His throne, and the counsel of peace will be between the two offices" (Zechariah 6:12,13).

Physically, it is not possible for one man to be both High Priest and King; kings were descended from the tribe of Judah, and priests were of the tribe of Levi. And for centuries the battle for leadership of God's people had gone on. Sometimes the High Priest was dominant, sometimes the king. With the coming of the Branch [Nazarene], as Zechariah had prophesied, as both High Priest and King, there would be the counsel of peace between the two offices.

Phase 5

Phase 5 in the Biblical plan is the birth, life, death, and resurrection of Jesus in accordance with all the Old Testament prophecies. The person of the *Messiah*, and His crucifixion and glorification are the central points of the whole Bible. These events were predicted in the Old Testament, and were covered in the previous section on prophecies of the Messiah.

Phase 6

Phase 6 was the establishment of the church, the kingdom of God. This was the fulfillment of Old Testament prophecies concerning the kingdom and the new covenant.

The purpose of the church was to take the "good news" of salvation to the Jews first. Man lost his fellowship with God through Adam's sin in the Garden of Eden, and by his own personal guilt. This fellowship with God is restored through the reconciliation which is available only through Jesus Christ (II Corinthians 5:18,19). By being "born of water and Spirit" (John 3:5) through immersion in Jesus' name (Acts 2:38), the Jew received the promise of fellowship with God through the Holy Spirit (Acts 2:39), which met his deepest need, and which had been unavailable until the coming of the Holy Spirit on the day of Pentecost, AD 30.

Most Jews rejected this covenant, preferring to look for a kingdom of their own imagination, as Isaiah had prophesied, "Go and tell this people: 'Keep on listening, but do not perceive; keep on looking, but do not understand' " (Isaiah 6:9).

But for those Jews who turned to Christ (descended from Abraham), fellowship with God was restored, and a portion of God's plan to bless all families through Abraham was fulfilled.

Phase 7

Phase 7 was the extension of salvation to the Gentiles some ten years

29

following the establishment of the church. This was really contrary to Jewish thinking, but was carefully laid out by God in His Plan centuries earlier when He promised Abraham that through him all families of earth would be blessed. As He explained in Hosea: "And it will come about that, in the place where it is said to them, 'You are not My people,' it will be said to them, 'You are the sons of the living God' " (Hosea 1:10). The Gentiles, who were not God's people under the terms of Mosaic Law, were to be the people of God [by faith] under the terms of the covenant yet to come. As the prophet Joel had spoken: "And it will come about that *whoever* calls upon the name of the Lord will be delivered [saved]" (Joel 2:32). *Whoever* includes Gentile as well as Jew!

The central theme of the New Testament is the need for teaching, exhorting, and edifying the church. And the reason for this is that the church is to carry out God's Plan for taking the message of salvation to all those in every nation—to whoever will call on the name of the Lord.

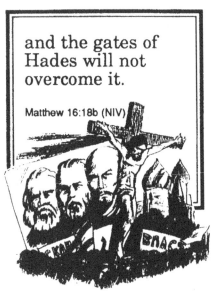

and the gates of Hades will not overcome it.

Matthew 16:18b (NIV)

Notice how this Phase of the Plan binds the Old and the New Testaments together as one single unit, committed to one purpose of seeking and saving the lost, who have been separated from the fellowship of God as a result of their own sin. It is revealed by Abraham's time that God is committed to blessing all those of every nation who will turn to Him; yet because of the nature of man, it was necessary to carry out His Plan in various stages. The New Testament church is the consummation of His Plan on earth; and it is clear that the instructions to the church are a vital part of the Bible.

It has been said: "The Old Testament is the New Testament concealed;

the New Testament is the Old Testament revealed." The Plan is contained, in a somewhat hidden fashion, in the Old Testament. It is clearly revealed in the New Testament.

Phase 8

Phase 8 of the Plan is not yet in effect. Phase 8 is the Judgment of God, foretold in both the Old and New Testaments. For those who have not met God's requirements, there is the eternal lake of fire; for those who have, there is eternal life. From the Old Testament: " 'For behold, the day is coming, burning like a furnace; and all the arrogant and every evildoer will be chaff; and the day that is coming will set them ablaze,' says the Lord of hosts, 'so that it will leave them neither root nor branch. But for you who fear My name the sun of righteousness will rise with healing in its wings; and you will go forth and skip about like calves from the stall. And you will tread down the wicked, for they shall be ashes under the soles of your feet on the day which I am preparing,' says the Lord of hosts" (Malachi 4:1–3). And from the New Testament: "Therefore having overlooked the times of ignorance, God is now declaring to men that all everywhere should repent, because He has fixed a day in which He will judge the world in righteousness through a Man whom He has appointed, *having furnished proof to all men by raising Him from the dead*" (Acts 17:30,31).

A Spiritual Building

The old homesteader's shack on the prairie is proof of the one-time existence of the homesteader. This evidence of design is proof of the operation of a human mind.

What do we see as we scan the prairies of history? We see, first of all, a few rough brush strokes of an idea emanating from a transcendent Mind in the antediluvian era. Following the Flood, the general idea is sketched out in Abraham's day. Then, beginning with the Mosaic Law, we see the Divine Architect earnestly, painstakingly, at the drafting table, laying out detail after detail in blueprint of the Old Testament.

Then, on the great and glorious day, we see the cornerstone (Jesus the

Messiah) of a spiritual building set carefully into place. Much detail in the Architectural drawings had gone into the cornerstone, and its being set into place was exuberantly celebrated.

Following the laying of the cornerstone, the foundation consisting of the apostles and the New Testament prophets was completed. The blueprint required that part of the foundation be Gentile as well as Jew, and it was with no small effort that suitable materials for the foundation were found. With the laying of the foundation, the building has continued in its construction, and when the last living stone is set in place, then the Designer will move in, that He might fill all in all.

As a physical building, built over a period of weeks or months, is proof of the existence of a human mind, so the erection of a spiritual building over a period of thousands of years is proof of the existence of a Divine Mind. And, as a set of blueprints for a building, found inside that structure, prove that the blueprints and the building itself are the result of the operation of one mind, so the Old and New Testaments may be shown to be the product of one Mind, and thus one inseparable unit. The prophecies of history essentially prove that the Old Testament is the word of God. The prophecies of the Messiah establish that Matthew through John is the word of God. And prophecies of the church, the spiritual building, prove that Acts through Revelation is the word of God.

On that basis, we submit to you that we have proven our contention that the Bible is in fact the word of God. Our case, we admit, in this booklet is but a kernel of what could be presented. But the towering oak of evidence which would constitute detailed and all-encompassing proof would only be the extension of those ideas which are contained in this seed. To the reasonable mind, our case is at this point settled.

Summary

It is clearly, and in successive detail, revealed in the Bible what God's Plan is. It is clear from the earliest times that the Plan is to save "whoever will" turn to Him with an honest heart. God used the Jewish nation to foreshadow the coming church, the church being the means which He is using to carry out His Plan to the ends of the earth. The Day of Judgment will be the final phase of the Plan, with its respective rewards.

The Plan is proof that the hand of God is in the whole Bible. The Plan is proof of the existence of a supernatural Designer. The Plan, relentlessly carried out in successive stages from Genesis through Revelation, makes it clear that both the Old and New Testaments are one unit, written by one Author, dictated through 40 different men over a span of 1500 years. The unity of The Plan requires that we accept the whole Bible as being what it claims to be, the inspired word of God. "All scripture is inspired by God and profitable for teaching, for reproof, for correction, for training in righteousness . . ." (II Timothy 3:16).

Summary of Internal Evidences

The proof that the Bible is the word of God comes from fulfilled prophecy. The prophecies of historical events, written hundreds of years before the history occurred, accurate down to fine details in many cases—including names—prove that the Author of the Bible is also the Author of history.

The prophecies of the Messiah, predicted in the Old Testament, add weight to the claim that the Bible is the word of God. The fact that the prophecies concerning the Messiah were clearly written prior to the coming of Jesus provides a crushing blow to claims that the prophecies in the Old Testament were written after the events prophesied occurred. The prophecies of Jesus begin building a bridge linking the Old Testament and the New.

Finally, the Plan—traced from Adam's fall in the Garden, through patriarchal sacrifices, through the Mosaic covenant, through the offering of Christ's blood and His resurrection, and His church and second coming for judgment—offers proof of a Supreme Mind which carries out His design through the centuries. The Plan not only offers proof of the existence of the Designer, but it completes the bridge between the Old and New Testaments, making it clear that they are component parts of one complete unit.

III. THE CONCLUSION

The Bible is the word of God for these two reasons:

1. The Bible is accurate in dealing with external matters. It is accurate in its record of archeology and natural science. In order to be the word of God, the Bible must be accurate in its portrayal of observable facts. The Bible meets this requirement of accuracy in external matters, and therefore can be the written revelation from God.

2. The proof that the Bible is the word of God comes from its internal contents. The Bible contains the following categories of internal evidence which prove it to be the word of God:

   a) Fulfilled historical prophecies.

   b) Fulfilled predictions of the Messiah.

   c) A Plan revealed, then carefully carried out—proof of the existence of the Planner, and a bridge binding the Old and New Testaments together as one complete unit.

For more information about Bible Creation and the Flood:

RECOMMENDED
ADDITIONAL RESOURCES

The Genesis Flood

Henry Morris and John Whitcomb. This excellent book discusses uniformitarianism, showing why catastrophism is the only plausible explanation of the earth's present landforms. Shows why the earth's testimony of its world–wide flood must be believed by any objective student.

Scientific Creationism

Edited by Henry M. Morris, developed as a textbook. Sets forth both creation and evolution models for the development of life, and shows in clear, understandable terms the superiority of creation over evolution as an explanation of the earth's life forms based on scientific data. Explodes the myths surrounding uranium decay into lead as a means of determining the age of fossils and rocks. Examines mutation, random action, and other subjects relating to evolutionary thought. This book is a must for the serious questioner.

Man's Origin, Man's Destiny

A.E. Wilder–Smith, 320 pages. In depth examination of evolution. Excellent pictures documenting dinosaur and man tracks in the Paluxy River.

Taylor Trail Photo Gallery

Don Patton, Ph.D., maintains a website with links to several images of dinosaur tracks in the Paluxy River in Glen Rose, Texas. Some of his images also show consecutive left/right human tracks in the same strata and even crossing the dinosaur tracks. www.bible.ca.

Origins—How the World Came to Be

This series of six videos featuring A.E. Wilder–Smith provides scientific evidence for Creation. Produced by Eden Communications. www.eden.org.

The Intelligent Design Collection

Illustra Media explores the foundations of intelligent design theory in three documentaries. www.illustramedia.com

Targeting Biblical Truth

This series by Luke Wilson offers several short videos related to the Bible and science, historical prophecies, and prophecies of the Christ. Available for free on youtube.com.

New Creation Study Series

The Personal Bible Study Series—A Track to Run on has been adapted to multiple PowerPoint presentations that incorporate pictures and highlight points from the series. Available at www.newcreation.us.

We Walked Where Dinosaurs Walked

by Jay Wilson

When we left Ft. Worth early that Saturday morning, we weren't sure what we would find. We were excited, though, because we had seen the movie *Footprints in Stone* previously, and our curiosity was running high.

As a child I had been interested in dinosaurs ever since I was old enough to read. My curiosity had led me to become familiar with the "theoretical rockpile," to recognize Madison limestone, to look for the "index fossil." And now I was going to the only place in the world where fossilized footprints of the giant Brontosaurus had been found (some of which have been removed and placed in New York's Museum of Natural History).

But what intrigued me more than even Brontosaurus tracks now was the prospect of seeing with my own eyes fossilized *human tracks* in the same sediments as the dinosaur tracks. I already had sufficient documentation on their existence, and their being in the same sedimentary rock as the

Photograph of Paluxy River bed. Stratum in which both human and dinosaur tracks are found is in the foreground (labeled "1"). Note the layers of limestone and other sedimentary rock ("2") which overlay the stratum in which fossil footprints are found.

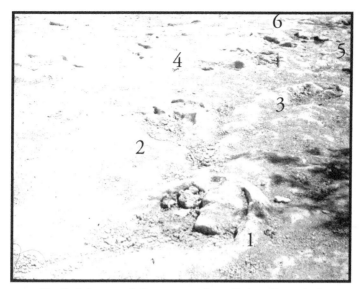

Trail of three-toed dinosaur tracks in Paluxy River bed.

dinosaur tracks, but I wanted to see them with my own eyes.

After little more than an hour's drive from Ft. Worth, we arrived at Dinosaur State Park, just past Glen Rose, Texas. Parking our car next to the Paluxy River bed, we climbed out into the heat, and scrambled to get to the river. The river was dry. It had been so hot and dry that the only water in the river was in a few deep holes; there was none flowing. So we started to walk down the dry river bed.

We found a few three-toed dinosaur tracks at first, but nothing spectacular. We continued to walk down the river for a mile and a half. There we found a set of dinosaur tracks crossing (from our perspective in time) the river. These three-toed tracks were about 18 inches across, and were roughly six feet apart. They looked like they were made in fresh mud, but what was once mud was now hard rock.

Then we found something really exciting! About 30 feet down river from the dinosaur tracks, in the same sediment, we found a giant man track! It was set deep in the mud (now hard rock) and was about a foot and a half long. The track was clearly human. It was a right footprint—the outline was clear; the heel, the instep, the toes were distinctly human. Not only that, but the big toe was so unmistakable that you could almost see the swirl of the toe print.

I was impressed. I had read the accounts of others who had documented the existence of human tracks with the dinosaur tracks. But here I was, seeing it for myself. From where I was standing, next to the huge man track, I could easily see the dinosaur tracks just ten yards away. I checked to see if there had been a change in sedimentary layers. But, no, the human track was in the same sediment as the dinosaur tracks. Here it was—*unmistakable proof that man and dinosaur lived at the same time*!

After lunch we decided to go up river. Our first find was some Brontosaurus tracks. They were unbelievable. The clearest showed the four claw marks in what is now solid rock. The track was almost three feet wide, two and one-half feet long, and about a foot deep into the mud. What a hulk that one must have been!Up river from the Brontosaurus tracks we found some more three-toed Tyrannosaurus tracks. They were much larger than the three-toed tracks we had found before lunch, and there was a fairly long trail of them going up river. As we followed them, we noticed how the mud had squished up in front of the dinosaur as he walked. No erosion marks could look like these.

Tyrannosaurus tracks going up river. Children are positioned next to tracks showing length of stride (about 10 ft.). Human tracks, not visible in this photo, are found next to the boy on the left and at the feet of the woman on the right.

Then we found them—a set of human tracks coming down river along side and crossing the dinosaur tracks!

These were smaller that the one we had seen in the morning; they were about the size of my wife's feet. One of the tracks, a right foot imprint, showed how the individual had slipped sideways in the mud. The heel and instep were extremely clear. In fact, there was still a slight overhang where the person had pulled his foot out of the mud, and the mud had not completely fallen

38

back in before the track was fossilized. No erosion mark could look like this.

About ten feet further on, the human tracks crossed the dinosaur tracks. Next to one of the dinosaur tracks a left footprint followed by a right footprint were clearly identifiable, with clear toe marks in the right footprint. Again, *unmistakable proof that man and dinosaurs had lived at the same time!*

We climbed back into the car. The 110° heat had pretty well drained us. It had been difficult walking down the bed of the Paluxy. We had explored all day, and had been able to cover (and not completely at that) two miles of river bottom.

Man tracks in the Paluxy. Water-filled pool in lower left is the dinosaur track next to the boy on the left on the previous page. These tracks (labeled "1" and "2") are clearly human, especially the right footprint ("2"). These are the same size as the author's wife's.

Although I was glad that I had seen the footprints myself, I realized that in order to do a really effective job, a person would have to spend months and years with a lot of equipment. And that of course is what was done to produce the documentary film *Footprints in Stone*, unfortunately no longer available.

Right foot human print, with shadows showing several inches indentation

into hardened mud. Toe marks along the right of print clearly show five toe prints; heel and instep are clear also. This print was located about 10 yards from a trail of three-toed dinosaur prints.

Proof that the Bible is the Word of God

Instructions: This set of questions is divided into two sections—Specific Questions and General Questions. The specific questions bring out many details in the study, and help you to understand many of the important points, and where in the scripture to find answers to common questions. The general questions help you to pick out the major ideas and concepts in the study. You may use your Bible and the study booklet for the Specific Questions, but try to answer the General Questions from memory.

Each section is divided into subsections, each of which has its own type of questions and its attendant instructions.

Specific Questions

Multiple Choice. More than one answer may be correct; show all correct answers.

_____ 1. Archeology is the study of:
   a) Human arches
   b) Human civilization
   c) Life
   d) Progressive development of primates

_____ 2. The story of Joshua and the battle of Jericho is recorded in:
   a) Judges 6
   b) Joshua 6
   c) Romans 6
   d) Moses 6

_____ 3. The men of Israel marched around Jericho:
   a) Once a day for six days
   b) Seven times on the seventh day
   c) Blowing trumpets
   d) In response to the command of God

41

4. The walls of Jericho fell down:
   a) During a Biblically recorded earthquake
   b) When the people shouted
   c) After the trumpets blew
   d) When they were burned

5. Evidence from *Halley's Bible Handbook*:
   a) Shows that the city of Jericho was burned
   b) Was taken from Dr. John Garstang
   c) Indicates the walls fell down flat
   d) Is usually reliable

6. Jericho:
   a) Is a mound with a city now existing on the top of it
   b) Was burned by the Israelites in 1400 BC
   c) Has been excavated to some extent
   d) Had a curse placed against the one who rebuilt it

7. Nineveh:
   a) Was a city with more than 120,000 small children
   b) Was built by Jonah
   c) Was the capital of the Assyrian Empire
   d) Was unknown to secular history until 1845

8. Within the city of Nineveh:
   a) Was the tower of Babel
   b) Was the "Yunas" Mound
   c) Flowed the Tigris River
   d) Was the library of Assurbanipal

9. The section on Archeology:
   a) Is part of Internal Evidences
   b) Uses two cities as representative of the Bible's accuracy in such matters
   c) Shows the Bible to be a collection of legends
   d) Draws information from *Halley's Bible Handbook*, available from Zondervan Press

_____ 10. Many other lost cities mentioned in the Bible have been found, including:

    a) Memphis

    b) Sidon

    c) Jerusalem

    d) Atlantis

Fill in the blanks.

The absence of historical and archeological _____
warrants the _____ that the Bible is more than a
collection of _____ .

Draw the evolutionary time chart in the space below. Show on the chart the evolutionist's estimation of the time of the extinction of trilobites and dinosaurs. Show when man came into existence, according to evolutionary thinking. Also, show the time chart according to creation.

Answer the following questions:

1. What three sections of scripture conclusively show that the Bible teaches that the earth and its initial inhabitants were created in six literal days.

    a)

    b)

    c)

2. Explain how dinosaur footprints fossilized in the same rock stratum as human footprints show that evolution is in error.

3. Evolutionary teaching is that an index fossil known as the trilobite died out some 300 million years ago. Show how the find of William Meister disproves that contention.

4. In the book *Scientific Creationism*, the following five points destroy the basis for evolutionary thinking in scientific circles:
   a)
   b)
   c)
   d)
   e)

5. Give the meaning of the Second Law of Thermodynamics in your own words. Then quote the Bible statement of the 2nd Law.

6. Is evolution a theory or a law?_____
   Explain the difference between a law and a theory.

True or False?

_____ 1. Proof that the Bible was written by God must be internal, because a man theoretically could write a book that is accurate in externals.

_____ 2. Fallen down buildings are not proof of the one-time existence of humans. Buildings can be built by animals or occur as a result of chance.

_____ 3. Internal proof that God exists is found in the Design which is blueprinted in the Old Testament and implemented in the New Testament.

_____ 4. Internal proofs connected with the Design are prophecies of history and the Messiah.

_____ 5. The Bible was written over a period of about 1500 years.

Multiple choice. More than one answer may be correct; show all correct answers.

_____ 1. Historical prophecies are:
   a) Predictions of events which will occur in the future
   b) Prophecies made when the prophet is extremely excited
   c) Guesses for money
   d) Sometimes apocalyptic

_____ 2. Examples of historical prophecy are:
   a) Naaman's dream
   b) Israel's leaving Egypt, prophesied to Abraham
   c) Israel's destruction by Assyria
   d) Prophecy of the Lamb and the Goat

_____ 3. Nebuchadnezzar's dream:
   a) Was given around 585 BC
   b) Was interpreted by the Chaldeans
   c) Consisted of a statue
   d) Upset the king greatly

_____ 4. Daniel:
   a) Would have been killed if he could not have interpreted the dream
   b) Appeared before the king
   c) Saw a statue smashed by a stone cut out of a mountain without human hands
   d) Interpreted the dream for the Persian king

_____ 5. The interpretation:
   a) Was given by astrologers
   b) Was sure
   c) Foretold the coming of four earthly kingdoms
   d) Was crushed

_____ 6. The stone that was cut out of the mountain without hands:
   a) Represented the church
   b) Was called the kingdom of God in Daniel 2:44
   c) Became a great mountain that filled the whole earth
   d) Occurred in the days of the iron kings, when the iron was mixed with clay

_____ 7. The four earthly kingdoms were:
   a) The Babylonians — gold
   b) The Greeks — silver
   c) The Persians — bronze
   d) The Romans — iron, iron mixed with clay

_____ 8. This prophecy:
   a) Was apocalyptic
   b) Occurred more than 200 years before the Greeks and 600 years before the church
   c) Is an example of apocalypses written after the events occurred
   d) Could easily be duplicated by man

Matching.

	Dream	**Interpretation**
_____	1. Daniel 8:1-8	a. Greece
_____	2. 545 BC	b. Medo-Persian Empire
_____	3. Ram	c. Four Generals
_____	4. Goat	d. Alexander the Great
_____	5. Large horn	e. Daniel 8:20-22
_____	6. 4 horns	f. Media-Persia
_____	7. North, west, south	g. 322 BC

Fill in the blank.

1. Isaiah lived and prophesied from _____ to _____ BC.

2. The Babylonians captured _____, the capital of Judah, in _____ BC.

3. Jerusalem was destroyed in 585 BC by the _____, and the only ones left alive were those who had been carried _____ to Babylon.

4. In _____ BC, the Persians, whose king was _____, conquered Babylon and allowed the captive peoples to return to their homelands.

5. Isaiah had prophesied, _____ years before the prophecy was fulfilled, the _____ of the Jews to Jerusalem and the rebuilding of the _____ under the direction of _____, king of Persia.

True or False.

_____ 1. Modern liberal scholars charge that the Bible has been doctored.

_____ 2. Modern liberal theology has endeavored to prove that the Old Testament is a compilation of material from four different sources, labeled "J", "E", "D", and "P".

_____ 3. There is considerable evidence, especially in the New Testament, that the Old Testament is inaccurate.

_____ 4. The accuracy of the historical prophecies of the Old Testament is not denied.

_____ 5. It is commonly taught on state university campuses across America that the historical prophecies were written after the events prophesied had already occurred.

Answer the following questions.

1. What does the word Messiah mean?

2. How did David become king?

3. List the eleven predictions of the Messiah found in Isaiah 53:
   a)

   b)

   c)

   d)

   e)

   f)

   g)

   h)

   i)

   j)

   k)

4. What is the central characteristic of the one described in Isaiah 53?

5. Could this section of scripture be applied to "comparatively inno-
    cent persons" who could suffer for the sake of others' sins? (Explain
    your answer.)

6. What does Psalm 22:16-18 describe?

    When was this written?

7. List seven details in the life of the Messiah foretold in the Old
    Testament:
    a)
    b)
    c)
    d)
    e)
    f)
    g)

Multiple choice. More than one answer may be correct; show all correct answers.

_____   1.   Isaiah 9:1,2:

           a)   Is quoted in Matthew 4:15,16
           b)   Prophesies Jesus' ministry in Galilee
           c)   Looks to the return of Zebulun and Naphtali
           d)   Was written in 530 BC

2. Psalm 16:8-10:

a) Refers to Jesus' ascension into heaven
b) Prophesies that He would not be long enough in the grave to see decay
c) Contains a reference to Sheol, which is the resting place for the souls of the dead
d) Prophesies that Jesus would sit at the right hand of the Father

3. Prophecies of the Messiah's birth:

a) Indicate that He would be born in Jerusalem
b) Clearly show that the Child is also the Father, Mighty God, and Wonderful Counselor
c) Predict His virgin birth
d) Describe Him as "God with us"

4. Prophecies of His kingdom include:

a) Isaiah 9:7
b) Zechariah 9:9
c) Alma 3:4
d) Habakkuk 5:7

5. Some of the 150 prophecies about the Jesus revealed in the New Testament are:

a) Psalm 110:4
b) Jeremiah 31:22
c) Zechariah 6:12,13
d) II Samuel 7:12-16

List the eight phases of the Plan.

    1.

    2.

    3.

    4.

    5.

    6.

    7.

    8.

Answer the following questions.

1. What is the lesson, for us, of Phase 1?

2. How does Phase 2 show the careful planning of God in His blueprint for the ages?

3. Describe the three ways in which Phase 3 clearly indicated the coming of the church.

    a)

    b)

    c)

Explain why it is important that these three aspects be foreshadowed in the Old Testament in order for the third Phase of the Plan to be significant.

4. What is the significance of Phase 4?

5. What is the importance of Phase 5?

6. How does Phase 6 relate back to the Garden of Eden?

7. How does Phase 7 differ from Phase 6?

Use Genesis 12:3, Hosea 1:10, and Joel 2:32 to explain the meaning of Ephesians 3:1-7.

8. What is the significance of Phase 8?

9. By comparing the Plan to a building, show how the Plan proves the existence of God, and how it binds the Old and New Testaments together as one complete unit.

_____ 1. Prophecies of the Messiah were clearly written before Christ came.

_____ 2. Historical prophecy has strong claim to being written before the events occurred because of the weight of Messianic prophecy.

_____ 3. The central feature of the Plan revealed throughout the Bible is the church.

_____ 4. It was clearly revealed in the Old Testament that Gentiles could not ever become a part of God's people.

_____ 5. Zechariah prophesied the coming of a man who would be both High Priest and King.

_____ 6. David is a foreshadow of the Messiah.

_____ 7. The prophesied High Priest would be an eternal High Priest of the order of Melchizedek.

_____ 8. The religion given through Moses was designed to last forever.

_____ 9. The church was only for the Jews and their relatives, the Samaritans, at first.

_____ 10. The church began to fulfill the words of Joel in Joel 2:32 and the words of Peter in Acts 2:39 when salvation went to the Gentiles in Phase 7.

_____ 11. Ephesians 2:19-22 describes the church as a building.

_____ 12. Salvation for the Gentiles was prophesied in God's word to Abraham in Phase 2 of God's Plan.

_____ 13. The death, burial, and resurrection of the Messiah were foretold in the Old Testament.

_____ 14. All scripture is inspired by God and is profitable for doctrine, for reproof, for correction, and for training in righteousness.

_____ 15. The Old Testament is the New Testament revealed, and the New Testament is the Old Testament concealed.

_____ 16. Proof of the coming of Phase 8 is the resurrection of Jesus.

_____ 17. The existence of a physical building is proof of the existence of a man. The existence of a spiritual building is proof of the existence of a Spiritual Being.

_____ 18. The church was blueprinted in Old Testament type and prophecy, and was built in the New Testament according to the Old Testament blueprint. The fact that this whole process is carried out over 1500 years is proof of the existence of a Divine Architect, and proof that the Bible is one complete unit.

General Questions

Fill in the blanks (do from memory).

1. This lesson is divided into two major sections:

   _____ _____ and

   _____ _____ .

2. Archeology and _____ _____ constitute the major divisions in _____

   _____ .

3. There are three major sections in Internal Evidences. These are:

   a)

   b)

   c)

4. The Bible must be true in _____ considerations, but this does not guarantee that it is the word of God.

5. Proof that the Bible is the word of God comes from

   _____ _____ which cannot be duplicated by mere men.

55

6. The Bible is the major guide to the great _____ finds of the Middle East because of its accuracy in such matters.

7. One of the great stumbling blocks to many people in believing the Bible is the _____ _____ .

8. The facts of science are more consistent with the Bible record of _____ than with the theory of _____ .

9. Prophecy consists of _____ of the future contained in written or spoken messages by preachers.

10. There are two major classifications of prophecy in this lesson; _____ prophecy, and predictions of the _____ .

11. The Hebrew word *Messiah* and its Greek equivalent *Christ* both mean "_____ _____ _____" .

12. Three representative historical prophecies discussed in this lesson are:

   a)

   b)

   c)

13. Liberal and conservative scholars alike often stumble over the Biblical fact that the kingdom of God is the _____ .

14. Clear evidence that the Old Testament, including Isaiah and Daniel, was written at the very least 100 years before Christ, comes from the _____ _____ _____ .

15. There are more than _____ specific prophecies of the Messiah in the Old Testament.

16. Prophecies of the Messiah include:

   a) His _____

b) His _____

c) His _____

d) His _____

e) His _____

17. Two very important and clear prophecies of the Messiah are found in Psalm 22 and _____ _____ .

18. There are _____ Phases to "The Plan."

19. The central feature of "The Plan" is the _____ which is blueprinted in the Old Testament and carried out in the New Testament.

20. _____ _____ completes the bridge between the Old and New Testaments and binds them together as one complete unit.

Made in the USA
Monee, IL
26 July 2024

62696109R00039